Computerised Accounting Practice Set Using Reckon Accounts

Expert Level

This expert level computerised accounting practice set is for students who need to practice exercises of Reckon Accounts software, students can record a month's transactions of Richmond Papers Pty Ltd and can create financial reports.

It covers the following topics.

a) Setting Up a New Accounting System
b) Integrated Business Transactions
c) Bank Reconciliation
d) Financial Reports

ESSTEE
BOOKS

Syed Tirmizi

Certified Advisor

ISBN 978-0-9945988-9-9

9 780994 598899 >

Part A

Practice Set

This page is blank.

Instructions

You have recently been appointed as an Accounts Assistant at Richmond Papers Pty Ltd, a new business dealing in printing and publishing. Your responsibilities are to set up a computerised accounting system, update the company records and produce financial reports.

The company started trading on 1st April 2016. All documents have been checked for accuracy and owner of the business, John Smith has authorised these documents.

The company uses straight line method for depreciating its non-current assets at 10% yearly. The policy defines the decline in value of these non-current assets on monthly basis.

You are required to complete the following tasks for April 2016 in the order given.

- a) Setting Up a New Accounting System
- b) Integrated Business Transactions
- c) Bank Reconciliation
- d) Financial Reports

a) Setting Up a New Accounting System

Create a new company in Reckon Accounts using the following information.

Setup Interview	
Company Name	Richmond Papers Pty Ltd
Tax ID	ACN995263632
Address	23 High Street
City	Richmond
State and Post Code	VIC 3121
Phone	03 9876 5432
Industry	Product Sales/Retail
Business Entity	Company Tax Return
Financial year starts in	July
Services or Products	Products only
Track Tax	Yes
Use Sales Receipts	Yes
Use Billing Statements	Yes
Use Invoices	Yes
Keep Track of Bills	Yes
Track Inventory	Yes
Employees	Yes
Date to Start Tracking	01-04-2016
Add Bank Account	Yes
Bank Account Details	Richmond Papers Pty Ltd – 987654321, Opened on 01-04-2016

Set up Chart of Accounts, Suppliers, Customers and Items with the help of Tables 1, 2, 3 and 4.

Additional Information

i.   On April 1st 2016, $25,000 Capital was introduced by the owner of the business in the form of cheque and was paid into the Bank Current Account. The cheque number is 067854.

ii.   On April 2nd 2016, the Company purchased a motor vehicle from Western Motors for $12,000 + $1,200 GST. Cheque number 000001 was used to make the settlement. Tax code is NCG.

iii.   At the end of the month depreciation on the motor vehicle and bank service charges are to be recorded to the relevant accounts.

Table 1: Chart of Accounts

To set up chart of accounts as given below you may need to add or edit accounts as necessary. Make sure that all accumulated depreciation accounts are set up as subaccount of the relevant fixed asset account.

Type of Account	Account Name
Bank	Richmond Papers Pty Ltd
Account Receivable	Trade Receivables
Other Current Asset	Inventory Asset
Fixed Asset	Motor Vehicle at Cost
Fixed Asset	Less Accum. Depr. Motor Vehicle
Account Payable	Trade Creditors
Other Current Liability	Bank Loan
Other Current Liability	Tax Payable
Equity	Owner's Capital
Income	Sales – A3 Copy Paper
Income	Sales – A4 Copy Paper
Income	Sales – A5 Copy Paper
Income	Sales – Coloured Paper
Income	Sales – Envelopes
Income	Sales – Register Rolls
Cost of Goods Sold	Cost of Goods Sold
Expense	Waste Disposals
Expense	Depreciation – Motor Vehicle
Expense	Electricity
Expense	Insurance
Expense	Interest Expense & Bank Charges
Expense	Rent
Expense	Bank Service Fee
Expense	Telephone

Table 2: Suppliers

Name	Account No.	Address	Credit Limit
Mark & Tony	MARKA001	41 Middleborough Road, St Albans, VIC 3021	$10,000
Terms	Tax Code	Tax Reg. ID	Country
Net 30	NCG	ACN678592583	Australia

Name	Account No.	Address	Credit Limit
David & Sons	DAVID001	67 Longwood Road, Craigieburn, VIC 3064	$15,000
Terms	Tax Code	Tax Reg. ID	Country
Net 30	NCG	ACN473985624	Australia

Name	Account No.	Address	Credit Limit
Ian & Co. Pty Ltd	IANAN001	94 High Street, Fitzroy, VIC 3065	$10,000
Terms	Tax Code	Tax Reg. ID	Country
Net 30	NCG	ACN657917634	Australia

Name	Account No.	Address	Credit Limit
Smith & Baker	SMITH001	11 Westfield Road, Lalor, VIC 3075	$10,000
Terms	Tax Code	Tax Reg. ID	Country
Net 30	NCG	ACN637945746	Australia

Name	Account No.	Address	Credit Limit
Gary Corporation	GARYC001	94 Wellington Street, Preston, VIC 3072	$15,000
Terms	Tax Code	Tax Reg. ID	Country
Net 30	NCG	ACN325496324	Australia

Name	Account No.	Address	Credit Limit
East End Pty Ltd	EASTE001	34 Canterbury Road, Epping, VIC 3076	$10,000
Terms	Tax Code	Tax Reg. ID	Country
Net 30	NCG	ACN376843587	Australia

Table 3: Customers

Name	Account No.	Address	Credit Limit
Peter Electronics	PETER001	9 Western Avenue, Brooklyn, VIC 3012	$10,000
Terms	**Tax Code**	**Tax Reg. ID**	**Country**
Net 30	GST	ACN639846324	Australia

Name	Account No.	Address	Credit Limit
Western Estate Agents	WESTE001	362 High Street, Sunshine, VIC 3020	$10,000
Terms	**Tax Code**	**Tax Reg. ID**	**Country**
Net 30	GST	ACN528963764	Australia

Name	Account No.	Address	Credit Limit
Surf Stores	SURFS001	54 Dundee Street, Deer Park, VIC 3023	$10,000
Terms	**Tax Code**	**Tax Reg. ID**	**Country**
Net 30	GST	ACN768359862	Australia

Name	Account No.	Address	Credit Limit
Sally's Warehouse	SALLY001	12 Wood Street, Essendon, VIC 3040	$15,000
Terms	**Tax Code**	**Tax Reg. ID**	**Country**
Net 30	GST	ACN662485964	Australia

Name	Account No.	Address	Credit Limit
Horizon Designs	HORIZ001	32 Abbots Road, Broadmeadows, VIC 3047	$6,000
Terms	**Tax Code**	**Tax Reg. ID**	**Country**
Net 30	GST	ACN528972562	Australia

Name	Account No.	Address	Credit Limit
Thomson Clothings	THOMS001	84 Spring Street, Thomastown, VIC 3074	$5,000
Terms	**Tax Code**	**Tax Reg. ID**	**Country**
Net 30	GST	ACN635842321	Australia

Name	Account No.	Address	Credit Limit
Globe Travels Pty Ltd	GLOBE001	42 Barry Road, Melbourne, VIC 3000	$10,000
Terms	**Tax Code**	**Tax Reg. ID**	**Country**
Net 30	GST	ACN365412741	Australia

Name	Account No.	Address	Credit Limit
Tiffany Cakes	TIFFA001	36 High Road, Williamstown, VIC 3016	$10,000
Terms	**Tax Code**	**Tax Reg. ID**	**Country**
Net 30	GST	ACN635254524	Australia

Table 4: Items List

Profile	Item 1	Item 2	Item 3	Item 4	Item 5	Item 6
Type	Inventory Part	Inventory Part	Inventory Part	Inventory Part	Inventory Part	Inventory Part
Item Name/Number	A3CP	A4CP	A5CP	COLO	EN01	RR18
Amts Inc Tax	☑	☑	☑	☑	☑	☑
Buying Details						
Description	A3 Copy Paper	A4 Copy Paper	A5 Copy Paper	Coloured Paper	Envelopes Large	Register Rolls
Gross Cost	$25	$8	$8	$14	$22	$38
Purch Tax Code	NCG	NCG	NCG	NCG	NCG	NCG
COGS Account	Cost of Goods Sold	Cost of Goods Sold	Cost of Goods Sold	Cost of Goods Sold	Cost of Goods Sold	Cost of Goods Sold
Selling Details						
Description	A3 Copy Paper	A4 Copy Paper	A5 Copy Paper	Coloured Paper	Envelopes Large	Register Rolls
Gross Amt.	40	15	14	20	35	54
Tax Code	GST	GST	GST	GST	GST	GST
Income Account	Sales - A3 Copy Paper	Sales - A4 Copy Paper	Sales - A5 Copy Paper	Sales - Coloured Paper	Sales - Envelopes	Sales - Register Rolls

b) Suppliers, Purchases and Inventory

Enter the following purchase invoices and purchase returns into the computer.

Purchase Invoices

Date	Supplier	Supp. Inv.	Item	Description	Qty	Cost	Gross Amt Inc GST
April 2nd	Gary Corporation	412	A3CP	A3 Copy Paper	200	$25.00	$5,000.00
April 2nd	Smith & Baker	G/749	A5CP	A5 Copy Paper	250	$8.00	$2,000.00
April 4th	Ian & Co. Pty Ltd	00854	A4CP	A4 Copy Paper	500	$8.00	$4,000.00
April 5th	David & Sons	2016-18	RR18	Register Rolls	350	$38.00	$13,300.00
April 7th	Mark & Tony	A423	COLO	Coloured Paper	200	$14.00	$2,800.00
April 9th	East End Pty Ltd	EE2141	EN01	Envelopes Large	200	$22.00	$4,400.00

Purchase Returns

Date	Supplier	Supp. Inv.	Item	Description	Qty	Cost	Gross Amt Inc GST
April 4th	Smith & Baker	G/749	A5CP	A5 Copy Paper	20	$8.00	$160.00
April 11th	David & Sons	2016-18	RR18	Register Rolls	25	$38.00	$950.00

c) Customers, Sales and Inventory

Enter the following sales invoices and sales returns into the computer.

Sales Invoices

Date	Customer	Doc. No.	Item	Description	Qty	Price	Amount Inc GST
April 5th	Horizon Designs	1	A4CP	A4 Copy Paper	70	$14.50	$1,015.00
			RR18	Register Rolls	60	$54.00	$3,240.00
			A5CP	A5 Copy Paper	70	$14.00	$980.00
						Total	$5,235.00
April 10th	Thomson Clothings	2	A4CP	A4 Copy Paper	60	$15.00	$900.00
			EN01	Envelopes Large	80	$35.00	$2,800.00
						Total	$3,700.00
April 12th	Globe Travels Pty Ltd	3	A4CP	A4 Copy Paper	60	$15.00	$900.00
			A3CP	A3 Copy Paper	50	$40.00	$2,000.00
			RR18	Register Rolls	70	$54.00	$3,780.00
			COLO	Coloured Paper	60	$20.00	$1,200.00
						Total	$7,880.00
April 14th	Tiffany Cakes	4	A4CP	A4 Copy Paper	50	$15.00	$750.00
			RR18	Register Rolls	60	$54.00	$3,240.00
			EN01	Envelopes Large	60	$35.00	$2,100.00
						Total	$6,090.00
April 19th	Peter Electronics	5	A4CP	A4 Copy Paper	60	$15.00	$900.00
			COLO	Coloured Paper	70	$20.00	$1,400.00
						Total	$2,300.00
April 21st	Sally's Warehouse	6	A4CP	A4 Copy Paper	70	$15.00	$1,050.00
			COLO	Coloured Paper	60	$20.00	$1,200.00
			A3CP	A3 Copy Paper	70	$40.00	$2,800.00
			RR18	Register Rolls	50	$54.00	$2,700.00
						Total	$7,750.00
April 25th	Western Estate Agents	7	A5CP	A5 Copy Paper	100	$14.00	$1,400.00
						Total	$1,400.00
April 27th	Surf Stores	8	A4CP	A4 Copy Paper	50	$15.00	$750.00
			RR18	Register Rolls	30	$54.00	$1,620.00
						Total	$2,370.00

Sales Returns

Date	Customer	Doc. No.	Item	Description	Qty	Price	Amount Inc GST
April 17th	Thomson Clothings	R1	EN01	Envelopes Large	20	$35.00	$700.00
April 23rd	Sally's Warehouse	R2	A4CP	A4 Copy Paper	10	$15.00	$150.00

d) Receipts, Payments and Expenses

Enter the following payments received from customers, payments made to suppliers and expenses into the computer.

Payments Received

Date	Receipt Type	Customer	Details	Amount ($)
April 13th	EFT	Horizon Designs	Invoice 1	$5,235.00
April 18th	Cheque	Thomson Clothings	Invoice 2	$3,000.00
April 20th	Cheque	Globe Travels Ltd	Invoice 3	$7,880.00
April 25th	EFT	Tiffany Cakes	Invoice 4	$6,090.00

Expenses Summary

Date	Cheque No.	Expenses	Details	Net	Tax	Gross ($)
April 2nd	000002	Rent	Richmond Real Estate	$1,000.00	$100.00	$1,100.00
April 7th	000003	Insurance Premium	Melbourne Insurance	$200.00	$20.00	$220.00
April 19th	000004	Electricity Bill	Victoria Electricity	$176.73	$17.67	$194.40
April 21st	000005	Telephone Bill	Australia Telecom	$196.92	$19.62	$215.84
April 26th	000006	Cleaning	Melbourne Removals	$50.00	$5.00	$55.00

Payments Made

Date	Cheque No.	Supplier	Details	Amount ($)
April 28th	000007	Gary Corporation	412	$5,000.00
April 28th	000008	Smith & Baker	G/749	$1,840.00

e) Bank Reconciliation

Prepare bank reconciliation for the month of April 2016. Company bank statement is as follows.

BANK OF RICHMOND

36 Spring Street, Richmond, VIC 3121

TEL 1800 AUSTRALIA

Cheque Account Statement

30-04-2016

Richmond Papers Pty Ltd
23 High Street
Richmond
VIC 3121

BSB Number	Account Number
123-456	987654321

Date	Details	Ref	Withdrawal	Deposits	Balance
01-Apr-16	Account opened - Initial deposit			$25,000.00	$25,000.00
02-Apr-16	CHQ 000001		$13,200.00		$11,800.00
02-Apr-16	CHQ 000002		$1,100.00		$10,700.00
07-Apr-16	CHQ 000003		$220.00		$10,480.00
13-Apr-16	EFT – Horizon Designs			$5,235.00	$15,715.00
18-Apr-16	Cheque deposited			$3,000.00	$18,715.00
19-Apr-16	CHQ 000004		$194.40		$18,520.60
20-Apr-16	Cheque deposited			$7,880.00	$26,400.60
21-Apr-16	CHQ 000005		$215.84		$26,184.76
22-Apr-16	CHQ 000007		$5,000.00		$21,184.76
25-Apr-16	EFT – Tiffany Cakes			$6,090.00	$27,274.76
30-Apr-16	Bank charges		$10.00		$27,264.76
	Totals		**$19,930.24**	**$47,205.00**	

d) Financial Reports

Print or save the following reports for the month of April 2016.

I.	Cheque Account Reconciliation
II.	General Ledger Report (In Use)
III.	Customer Balance Detail
IV.	Supplier Balance Detail
V.	Inventory Valuation Detail
VI.	Expenses by Supplier Detail
VII.	Statement of Cash Flows
VIII.	Trial Balance
IX.	Profit and Loss Detail
X.	Balance Sheet

Part B

Solutions

This page is blank.

Richmond Papers Pty Ltd
Reconciliation Detail
Richmond Papers Pty Ltd, Period Ending 30-04-2016

Type	Date	Num	Name	Clr	Amount	Balance
Beginning Balance						0.00
Cleared Transactions						
Cheques and Payments - 7 items						
Cheque	02-Apr-2016	1	Western Motors	X	-13,200.00	-13,200.00
Cheque	02-Apr-2016	2	Richmond Real Estate	X	-1,100.00	-14,300.00
Cheque	07-Apr-2016	3	Melbourne Insurance	X	-220.00	-14,520.00
Cheque	19-Apr-2016	4	Victoria Electricity	X	-194.40	-14,714.40
Cheque	21-Apr-2016	5	Australia Telecom	X	-215.84	-14,930.24
Bill Pmt -Cheque	28-Apr-2016	7	Gary Corporation	X	-5,000.00	-19,930.24
Cheque	30-Apr-2016	BS	Bank of Richmond	X	-10.00	-19,940.24
Total Cheques and Payments					-19,940.24	-19,940.24
Deposits and Credits - 5 items						
Deposit	01-Apr-2016			X	25,000.00	25,000.00
Deposit	13-Apr-2016			X	5,235.00	30,235.00
Deposit	18-Apr-2016			X	3,000.00	33,235.00
Deposit	20-Apr-2016			X	7,880.00	41,115.00
Deposit	25-Apr-2016			X	6,090.00	47,205.00
Total Deposits and Credits					47,205.00	47,205.00
Total Cleared Transactions					27,264.76	27,264.76
Cleared Balance					27,264.76	27,264.76
Uncleared Transactions						
Cheques and Payments - 2 items						
Cheque	26-Apr-2016	6	Melbourne Removals		-55.00	-55.00
Bill Pmt -Cheque	28-Apr-2016	8	Smith & Baker		-1,840.00	-1,895.00
Total Cheques and Payments					-1,895.00	-1,895.00
Total Uncleared Transactions					-1,895.00	-1,895.00
Register Balance as of 30-04-2016					25,369.76	25,369.76
Ending Balance					**25,369.76**	**25,369.76**

Page 1

Richmond Papers Pty Ltd
General Ledger

Accrual Basis

As of April 30, 2016

Type	Date	Num	Name	Amount	Balance
Richmond Papers Pty Ltd					0.00
Deposit	01-Apr-2016			25,000.00	25,000.00
Cheque	02-Apr-2016	1	Western Motors	-13,200.00	11,800.00
Cheque	02-Apr-2016	2	Richmond Real Estate	-1,100.00	10,700.00
Cheque	07-Apr-2016	3	Melbourne Insurance	-220.00	10,480.00
Deposit	13-Apr-2016			5,235.00	15,715.00
Deposit	18-Apr-2016			3,000.00	18,715.00
Cheque	19-Apr-2016	4	Victoria Electricity	-194.40	18,520.60
Deposit	20-Apr-2016			7,880.00	26,400.60
Cheque	21-Apr-2016	5	Australia Telecom	-215.84	26,184.76
Deposit	25-Apr-2016			6,090.00	32,274.76
Cheque	26-Apr-2016	6	Melbourne Removals	-55.00	32,219.76
Bill Pmt -Cheque	28-Apr-2016	7	Gary Corporation	-5,000.00	27,219.76
Bill Pmt -Cheque	28-Apr-2016	8	Smith & Baker	-1,840.00	25,379.76
Cheque	30-Apr-2016	BS	Bank of Richmond	-10.00	25,369.76
Total Richmond Papers Pty Ltd				25,369.76	25,369.76
Trade receivables					0.00
Tax Invoice	05-Apr-2016	1	Horizon Designs	5,235.00	5,235.00
Tax Invoice	10-Apr-2016	2	Thomson Clothings	3,700.00	8,935.00
Tax Invoice	12-Apr-2016	3	Globe Travels Pty Ltd	7,880.00	16,815.00
Payment	13-Apr-2016	Invoice 1	Horizon Designs	-5,235.00	11,580.00
Tax Invoice	14-Apr-2016	4	Tiffany Cakes	6,090.00	17,670.00
Adjustment Note	17-Apr-2016	R1	Thomson Clothings	-700.00	16,970.00
Payment	18-Apr-2016	Invoice 2	Thomson Clothings	-3,000.00	13,970.00
Tax Invoice	19-Apr-2016	5	Peter Electronics	2,300.00	16,270.00
Payment	20-Apr-2016	Invoice 3	Globe Travels Pty Ltd	-7,880.00	8,390.00
Tax Invoice	21-Apr-2016	6	Sally's Warehouse	7,750.00	16,140.00
Adjustment Note	23-Apr-2016	R2	Sally's Warehouse	-150.00	15,990.00
Tax Invoice	25-Apr-2016	7	Western Estate Agents	1,400.00	17,390.00
Payment	25-Apr-2016	Invoice 4	Tiffany Cakes	-6,090.00	11,300.00
Tax Invoice	27-Apr-2016	8	Surf Stores	2,370.00	13,670.00
Total Trade receivables				13,670.00	13,670.00
Inventory Asset					0.00
Bill	02-Apr-2016	412	Gary Corporation	4,545.45	4,545.45
Bill	02-Apr-2016	G/749	Smith & Baker	1,818.18	6,363.63
Bill	04-Apr-2016	00854	Ian & Co. Pty Ltd	3,636.36	9,999.99
Credit	04-Apr-2016	G/749	Smith & Baker	-145.45	9,854.54
Bill	05-Apr-2016	2016-18	David & Sons	12,090.91	21,945.45
Tax Invoice	05-Apr-2016	1	Horizon Designs	-509.09	21,436.36
Tax Invoice	05-Apr-2016	1	Horizon Designs	-2,072.73	19,363.63
Tax Invoice	05-Apr-2016	1	Horizon Designs	-509.09	18,854.54
Bill	07-Apr-2016	A423	Mark & Tony	2,545.45	21,399.99
Bill	09-Apr-2016	EE2141	East End Pty Ltd	4,000.00	25,399.99
Tax Invoice	10-Apr-2016	2	Thomson Clothings	-436.36	24,963.63
Tax Invoice	10-Apr-2016	2	Thomson Clothings	-1,600.00	23,363.63
Credit	11-Apr-2016	2016-18	David & Sons	-863.64	22,499.99
Tax Invoice	12-Apr-2016	3	Globe Travels Pty Ltd	-436.36	22,063.63
Tax Invoice	12-Apr-2016	3	Globe Travels Pty Ltd	-1,136.36	20,927.27
Tax Invoice	12-Apr-2016	3	Globe Travels Pty Ltd	-2,418.18	18,509.09
Tax Invoice	12-Apr-2016	3	Globe Travels Pty Ltd	-763.64	17,745.45
Tax Invoice	14-Apr-2016	4	Tiffany Cakes	-363.64	17,381.81
Tax Invoice	14-Apr-2016	4	Tiffany Cakes	-2,072.73	15,309.08
Tax Invoice	14-Apr-2016	4	Tiffany Cakes	-1,200.00	14,109.08
Adjustment Note	17-Apr-2016	R1	Thomson Clothings	400.00	14,509.08
Tax Invoice	19-Apr-2016	5	Peter Electronics	-436.36	14,072.72
Tax Invoice	19-Apr-2016	5	Peter Electronics	-890.91	13,181.81
Tax Invoice	21-Apr-2016	6	Sally's Warehouse	-509.09	12,672.72
Tax Invoice	21-Apr-2016	6	Sally's Warehouse	-763.64	11,909.08
Tax Invoice	21-Apr-2016	6	Sally's Warehouse	-1,590.91	10,318.17
Tax Invoice	21-Apr-2016	6	Sally's Warehouse	-1,727.27	8,590.90
Adjustment Note	23-Apr-2016	R2	Sally's Warehouse	72.73	8,663.63
Tax Invoice	25-Apr-2016	7	Western Estate Agents	-727.27	7,936.36
Tax Invoice	27-Apr-2016	8	Surf Stores	-363.64	7,572.72
Tax Invoice	27-Apr-2016	8	Surf Stores	-1,036.36	6,536.36
Total Inventory Asset				6,536.36	6,536.36

Page 1

Richmond Papers Pty Ltd
General Ledger
As of April 30, 2016

Accrual Basis

Type	Date	Num	Name	Amount	Balance
Undeposited Funds					0.00
Payment	13-Apr-2016	Invoice 1	Horizon Designs	5,235.00	5,235.00
Deposit	13-Apr-2016		Horizon Designs	-5,235.00	0.00
Payment	18-Apr-2016	Invoice 2	Thomson Clothings	3,000.00	3,000.00
Deposit	18-Apr-2016		Thomson Clothings	-3,000.00	0.00
Payment	20-Apr-2016	Invoice 3	Globe Travels Pty Ltd	7,880.00	7,880.00
Deposit	20-Apr-2016		Globe Travels Pty Ltd	-7,880.00	0.00
Payment	25-Apr-2016	Invoice 4	Tiffany Cakes	6,090.00	6,090.00
Deposit	25-Apr-2016		Tiffany Cakes	-6,090.00	0.00
Total Undeposited Funds				0.00	0.00
Motor Vehicle at Cost					0.00
Less Accum. Depr. Motor Vehicle					0.00
General Journal	30-Apr-2016	1		-100.00	-100.00
Total Less Accum. Depr. Motor Vehicle				-100.00	-100.00
Motor Vehicle at Cost - Other					0.00
Cheque	02-Apr-2016	1	Western Motors	12,000.00	12,000.00
Total Motor Vehicle at Cost - Other				12,000.00	12,000.00
Total Motor Vehicle at Cost				11,900.00	11,900.00
Trade creditors					0.00
Bill	02-Apr-2016	412	Gary Corporation	-5,000.00	-5,000.00
Bill	02-Apr-2016	G/749	Smith & Baker	-2,000.00	-7,000.00
Bill	04-Apr-2016	00854	Ian & Co. Pty Ltd	-4,000.00	-11,000.00
Credit	04-Apr-2016	G/749	Smith & Baker	160.00	-10,840.00
Bill	05-Apr-2016	2016-18	David & Sons	-13,300.00	-24,140.00
Bill	07-Apr-2016	A423	Mark & Tony	-2,800.00	-26,940.00
Bill	09-Apr-2016	EE2141	East End Pty Ltd	-4,400.00	-31,340.00
Credit	11-Apr-2016	2016-18	David & Sons	950.00	-30,390.00
Bill Pmt -Cheque	28-Apr-2016	7	Gary Corporation	5,000.00	-25,390.00
Bill Pmt -Cheque	28-Apr-2016	8	Smith & Baker	1,840.00	-23,550.00
Total Trade creditors				-23,550.00	-23,550.00
Tax Payable					0.00
Cheque	02-Apr-2016	1	Australian Taxation Office	1,200.00	1,200.00
Bill	02-Apr-2016	412	Australian Taxation Office	454.55	1,654.55
Bill	02-Apr-2016	G/749	Australian Taxation Office	181.82	1,836.37
Cheque	02-Apr-2016	2	Australian Taxation Office	100.00	1,936.37
Bill	04-Apr-2016	00854	Australian Taxation Office	363.64	2,300.01
Credit	04-Apr-2016	G/749	Australian Taxation Office	-14.55	2,285.46
Bill	05-Apr-2016	2016-18	Australian Taxation Office	1,209.09	3,494.55
Tax Invoice	05-Apr-2016	1	Australian Taxation Office	-475.91	3,018.64
Bill	07-Apr-2016	A423	Australian Taxation Office	254.55	3,273.19
Cheque	07-Apr-2016	3	Australian Taxation Office	20.00	3,293.19
Bill	09-Apr-2016	EE2141	Australian Taxation Office	400.00	3,693.19
Tax Invoice	10-Apr-2016	2	Australian Taxation Office	-336.37	3,356.82
Credit	11-Apr-2016	2016-18	Australian Taxation Office	-86.36	3,270.46
Tax Invoice	12-Apr-2016	3	Australian Taxation Office	-716.37	2,554.09
Tax Invoice	14-Apr-2016	4	Australian Taxation Office	-553.64	2,000.45
Adjustment Note	17-Apr-2016	R1	Australian Taxation Office	63.64	2,064.09
Tax Invoice	19-Apr-2016	5	Australian Taxation Office	-209.09	1,855.00
Cheque	19-Apr-2016	4	Australian Taxation Office	17.67	1,872.67
Tax Invoice	21-Apr-2016	6	Australian Taxation Office	-704.54	1,168.13
Cheque	21-Apr-2016	5	Australian Taxation Office	19.62	1,187.75
Adjustment Note	23-Apr-2016	R2	Australian Taxation Office	13.64	1,201.39
Tax Invoice	25-Apr-2016	7	Australian Taxation Office	-127.27	1,074.12
Cheque	26-Apr-2016	6	Australian Taxation Office	5.00	1,079.12
Tax Invoice	27-Apr-2016	8	Australian Taxation Office	-215.45	863.67
General Journal	30-Apr-2016	1	Australian Taxation Office	0.00	863.67
Cheque	30-Apr-2016	BS	Australian Taxation Office	0.00	863.67
Total Tax Payable				863.67	863.67
Owner's Capital					0.00
Deposit	01-Apr-2016		John Smith	-25,000.00	-25,000.00
Total Owner's Capital				-25,000.00	-25,000.00
Sales - A3 Copy Paper					0.00
Tax Invoice	12-Apr-2016	3	Globe Travels Pty Ltd	-1,818.18	-1,818.18
Tax Invoice	21-Apr-2016	6	Sally's Warehouse	-2,545.45	-4,363.63
Total Sales - A3 Copy Paper				-4,363.63	-4,363.63

Page 2

Richmond Papers Pty Ltd
General Ledger
As of April 30, 2016

Accrual Basis

Type	Date	Num	Name	Amount	Balance
Sales - A4 Copy Paper					0.00
Tax Invoice	05-Apr-2016	1	Horizon Designs	-922.73	-922.73
Tax Invoice	10-Apr-2016	2	Thomson Clothings	-818.18	-1,740.91
Tax Invoice	12-Apr-2016	3	Globe Travels Pty Ltd	-818.18	-2,559.09
Tax Invoice	14-Apr-2016	4	Tiffany Cakes	-681.82	-3,240.91
Tax Invoice	19-Apr-2016	5	Peter Electronics	-818.18	-4,059.09
Tax Invoice	21-Apr-2016	6	Sally's Warehouse	-954.55	-5,013.64
Adjustment Note	23-Apr-2016	R2	Sally's Warehouse	136.36	-4,877.28
Tax Invoice	27-Apr-2016	8	Surf Stores	-681.82	-5,559.10
Total Sales - A4 Copy Paper				-5,559.10	-5,559.10
Sales - A5 Copy Paper					0.00
Tax Invoice	05-Apr-2016	1	Horizon Designs	-890.91	-890.91
Tax Invoice	25-Apr-2016	7	Western Estate Agents	-1,272.73	-2,163.64
Total Sales - A5 Copy Paper				-2,163.64	-2,163.64
Sales - Coloured Paper					0.00
Tax Invoice	12-Apr-2016	3	Globe Travels Pty Ltd	-1,090.91	-1,090.91
Tax Invoice	19-Apr-2016	5	Peter Electronics	-1,272.73	-2,363.64
Tax Invoice	21-Apr-2016	6	Sally's Warehouse	-1,090.91	-3,454.55
Total Sales - Coloured Paper				-3,454.55	-3,454.55
Sales - Envelopes					0.00
Tax Invoice	10-Apr-2016	2	Thomson Clothings	-2,545.45	-2,545.45
Tax Invoice	14-Apr-2016	4	Tiffany Cakes	-1,909.09	-4,454.54
Adjustment Note	17-Apr-2016	R1	Thomson Clothings	636.36	-3,818.18
Total Sales - Envelopes				-3,818.18	-3,818.18
Sales - Register Rolls					0.00
Tax Invoice	05-Apr-2016	1	Horizon Designs	-2,945.45	-2,945.45
Tax Invoice	12-Apr-2016	3	Globe Travels Pty Ltd	-3,436.36	-6,381.81
Tax Invoice	14-Apr-2016	4	Tiffany Cakes	-2,945.45	-9,327.26
Tax Invoice	21-Apr-2016	6	Sally's Warehouse	-2,454.55	-11,781.81
Tax Invoice	27-Apr-2016	8	Surf Stores	-1,472.73	-13,254.54
Total Sales - Register Rolls				-13,254.54	-13,254.54
Cost of Goods Sold					0.00
Tax Invoice	05-Apr-2016	1	Horizon Designs	509.09	509.09
Tax Invoice	05-Apr-2016	1	Horizon Designs	2,072.73	2,581.82
Tax Invoice	05-Apr-2016	1	Horizon Designs	509.09	3,090.91
Tax Invoice	10-Apr-2016	2	Thomson Clothings	436.36	3,527.27
Tax Invoice	10-Apr-2016	2	Thomson Clothings	1,600.00	5,127.27
Tax Invoice	12-Apr-2016	3	Globe Travels Pty Ltd	436.36	5,563.63
Tax Invoice	12-Apr-2016	3	Globe Travels Pty Ltd	1,136.36	6,699.99
Tax Invoice	12-Apr-2016	3	Globe Travels Pty Ltd	2,418.18	9,118.17
Tax Invoice	12-Apr-2016	3	Globe Travels Pty Ltd	763.64	9,881.81
Tax Invoice	14-Apr-2016	4	Tiffany Cakes	363.64	10,245.45
Tax Invoice	14-Apr-2016	4	Tiffany Cakes	2,072.73	12,318.18
Tax Invoice	14-Apr-2016	4	Tiffany Cakes	1,200.00	13,518.18
Adjustment Note	17-Apr-2016	R1	Thomson Clothings	-400.00	13,118.18
Tax Invoice	19-Apr-2016	5	Peter Electronics	436.36	13,554.54
Tax Invoice	19-Apr-2016	5	Peter Electronics	890.91	14,445.45
Tax Invoice	21-Apr-2016	6	Sally's Warehouse	509.09	14,954.54
Tax Invoice	21-Apr-2016	6	Sally's Warehouse	763.64	15,718.18
Tax Invoice	21-Apr-2016	6	Sally's Warehouse	1,590.91	17,309.09
Tax Invoice	21-Apr-2016	6	Sally's Warehouse	1,727.27	19,036.36
Adjustment Note	23-Apr-2016	R2	Sally's Warehouse	-72.73	18,963.63
Tax Invoice	25-Apr-2016	7	Western Estate Agents	727.27	19,690.90
Tax Invoice	27-Apr-2016	8	Surf Stores	363.64	20,054.54
Tax Invoice	27-Apr-2016	8	Surf Stores	1,036.36	21,090.90
Total Cost of Goods Sold				21,090.90	21,090.90
Bank Service Fee					0.00
Cheque	30-Apr-2016	BS	Bank of Richmond	10.00	10.00
Total Bank Service Fee				10.00	10.00
Depreciation – Motor Vehicle					0.00
General Journal	30-Apr-2016	1		100.00	100.00
Total Depreciation – Motor Vehicle				100.00	100.00

Richmond Papers Pty Ltd
General Ledger
As of April 30, 2016

Accrual Basis

Type	Date	Num	Name	Amount	Balance
Electricity					0.00
Cheque	19-Apr-2016	4	Victoria Electricity	176.73	176.73
Total Electricity				176.73	176.73
Insurance					0.00
Cheque	07-Apr-2016	3	Melbourne Insurance	200.00	200.00
Total Insurance				200.00	200.00
Rent					0.00
Cheque	02-Apr-2016	2	Richmond Real Estate	1,000.00	1,000.00
Total Rent				1,000.00	1,000.00
Telephone					0.00
Cheque	21-Apr-2016	5	Australia Telecom	196.22	196.22
Total Telephone				196.22	196.22
Waste disposal					0.00
Cheque	26-Apr-2016	6	Melbourne Removals	50.00	50.00
Total Waste disposal				50.00	50.00
TOTAL				**0.00**	**0.00**

Page 4

Richmond Papers Pty Ltd
Customer Balance Detail
All Transactions

Type	Date	Num	Account	Amount	Balance
Globe Travels Pty Ltd					
Tax Invoice	12-Apr-2016	3	Trade receivables	7,880.00	7,880.00
Payment	20-Apr-2016	Invoice 3	Trade receivables	-7,880.00	0.00
Total Globe Travels Pty Ltd				0.00	0.00
Horizon Designs					
Tax Invoice	05-Apr-2016	1	Trade receivables	5,235.00	5,235.00
Payment	13-Apr-2016	Invoice 1	Trade receivables	-5,235.00	0.00
Total Horizon Designs				0.00	0.00
Peter Electronics					
Tax Invoice	19-Apr-2016	5	Trade receivables	2,300.00	2,300.00
Total Peter Electronics				2,300.00	2,300.00
Sally's Warehouse					
Tax Invoice	21-Apr-2016	6	Trade receivables	7,750.00	7,750.00
Adjustment Note	23-Apr-2016	R2	Trade receivables	-150.00	7,600.00
Total Sally's Warehouse				7,600.00	7,600.00
Surf Stores					
Tax Invoice	27-Apr-2016	8	Trade receivables	2,370.00	2,370.00
Total Surf Stores				2,370.00	2,370.00
Thomson Clothings					
Tax Invoice	10-Apr-2016	2	Trade receivables	3,700.00	3,700.00
Adjustment Note	17-Apr-2016	R1	Trade receivables	-700.00	3,000.00
Payment	18-Apr-2016	Invoice 2	Trade receivables	-3,000.00	0.00
Total Thomson Clothings				0.00	0.00
Tiffany Cakes					
Tax Invoice	14-Apr-2016	4	Trade receivables	6,090.00	6,090.00
Payment	25-Apr-2016	Invoice 4	Trade receivables	-6,090.00	0.00
Total Tiffany Cakes				0.00	0.00
Western Estate Agents					
Tax Invoice	25-Apr-2016	7	Trade receivables	1,400.00	1,400.00
Total Western Estate Agents				1,400.00	1,400.00
TOTAL				**13,670.00**	**13,670.00**

Page 1

Richmond Papers Pty Ltd
Supplier Balance Detail
All Transactions

Type	Date	Num	Account	Amount	Balance
David & Sons					
Bill	05-Apr-2016	2016-18	Trade creditors	13,300.00	13,300.00
Credit	11-Apr-2016	2016-18	Trade creditors	-950.00	12,350.00
Total David & Sons				12,350.00	12,350.00
East End Pty Ltd					
Bill	09-Apr-2016	EE2141	Trade creditors	4,400.00	4,400.00
Total East End Pty Ltd				4,400.00	4,400.00
Gary Corporation					
Bill	02-Apr-2016	412	Trade creditors	5,000.00	5,000.00
Bill Pmt -Cheque	28-Apr-2016	7	Trade creditors	-5,000.00	0.00
Total Gary Corporation				0.00	0.00
Ian & Co. Pty Ltd					
Bill	04-Apr-2016	00854	Trade creditors	4,000.00	4,000.00
Total Ian & Co. Pty Ltd				4,000.00	4,000.00
Mark & Tony					
Bill	07-Apr-2016	A423	Trade creditors	2,800.00	2,800.00
Total Mark & Tony				2,800.00	2,800.00
Smith & Baker					
Bill	02-Apr-2016	G/749	Trade creditors	2,000.00	2,000.00
Credit	04-Apr-2016	G/749	Trade creditors	-160.00	1,840.00
Bill Pmt -Cheque	28-Apr-2016	8	Trade creditors	-1,840.00	0.00
Total Smith & Baker				0.00	0.00
TOTAL				**23,550.00**	**23,550.00**

Page 1

Richmond Papers Pty Ltd
Inventory Valuation Detail
April 2016

Type	Date	Name	Num	Qty	Cost	On Hand	Avg Cost	Asset Value
Inventory								
A3CP								
Bill	02-Apr-2016	Gary Corporation	412	200	4,545.45	200	22.73	4,545.45
Tax Invoice	12-Apr-2016	Globe Travels Pty Ltd	3	-50		150	22.73	3,409.09
Tax Invoice	21-Apr-2016	Sally's Warehouse	6	-70		80	22.73	1,818.18
Total A3CP						80.00		1,818.18
A4CP								
Bill	04-Apr-2016	Ian & Co. Pty Ltd	00854	500	3,636.36	500	7.27	3,636.36
Tax Invoice	05-Apr-2016	Horizon Designs	1	-70		430	7.27	3,127.27
Tax Invoice	10-Apr-2016	Thomson Clothings	2	-60		370	7.27	2,690.91
Tax Invoice	12-Apr-2016	Globe Travels Pty Ltd	3	-60		310	7.27	2,254.55
Tax Invoice	14-Apr-2016	Tiffany Cakes	4	-50		260	7.27	1,890.91
Tax Invoice	19-Apr-2016	Peter Electronics	5	-60		200	7.27	1,454.55
Tax Invoice	21-Apr-2016	Sally's Warehouse	6	-70		130	7.27	945.46
Adjustment Note	23-Apr-2016	Sally's Warehouse	R2	10		140	7.27	1,018.19
Tax Invoice	27-Apr-2016	Surf Stores	8	-50		90	7.27	654.55
Total A4CP						90.00		654.55
A5CP								
Bill	02-Apr-2016	Smith & Baker	G/749	250	1,818.18	250	7.27	1,818.18
Credit	04-Apr-2016	Smith & Baker	G/749	-20	-145.45	230	7.27	1,672.73
Tax Invoice	05-Apr-2016	Horizon Designs	1	-70		160	7.27	1,163.64
Tax Invoice	25-Apr-2016	Western Estate Agents	7	-100		60	7.27	436.37
Total A5CP						60.00		436.37
COLO								
Bill	07-Apr-2016	Mark & Tony	A423	200	2,545.45	200	12.73	2,545.45
Tax Invoice	12-Apr-2016	Globe Travels Pty Ltd	3	-60		140	12.73	1,781.81
Tax Invoice	19-Apr-2016	Peter Electronics	5	-70		70	12.73	890.90
Tax Invoice	21-Apr-2016	Sally's Warehouse	6	-60		10	12.73	127.26
Total COLO						10.00		127.26
EN01								
Bill	09-Apr-2016	East End Pty Ltd	EE2141	200	4,000.00	200	20.00	4,000.00
Tax Invoice	10-Apr-2016	Thomson Clothings	2	-80		120	20.00	2,400.00
Tax Invoice	14-Apr-2016	Tiffany Cakes	4	-60		60	20.00	1,200.00
Adjustment Note	17-Apr-2016	Thomson Clothings	R1	20		80	20.00	1,600.00
Total EN01						80.00		1,600.00
RR18								
Bill	05-Apr-2016	David & Sons	2016-18	350	12,090.91	350	34.55	12,090.91
Tax Invoice	05-Apr-2016	Horizon Designs	1	-60		290	34.55	10,018.18
Credit	11-Apr-2016	David & Sons	2016-18	-25	-863.64	265	34.55	9,154.54
Tax Invoice	12-Apr-2016	Globe Travels Pty Ltd	3	-70		195	34.55	6,736.36
Tax Invoice	14-Apr-2016	Tiffany Cakes	4	-60		135	34.55	4,663.63
Tax Invoice	21-Apr-2016	Sally's Warehouse	6	-50		85	34.55	2,936.36
Tax Invoice	27-Apr-2016	Surf Stores	8	-30		55	34.55	1,900.00
Total RR18						55.00		1,900.00
Total Inventory						375.00		6,536.36
TOTAL						**375.00**		**6,536.36**

Richmond Papers Pty Ltd
Expenses by Supplier Detail

Accrual Basis   April 2016

Type	Date	Num	Account	Clr	Amount	Balance
Australia Telecom						
Cheque	21-Apr-2016	5	Telephone		196.22	196.22
Total Australia Telecom					196.22	196.22
Bank of Richmond						
Cheque	30-Apr-2016	BS	Bank Service Fee		10.00	10.00
Total Bank of Richmond					10.00	10.00
Melbourne Insurance						
Cheque	07-Apr-2016	3	Insurance		200.00	200.00
Total Melbourne Insurance					200.00	200.00
Melbourne Removals						
Cheque	26-Apr-2016	6	Waste disposal		50.00	50.00
Total Melbourne Removals					50.00	50.00
Richmond Real Estate						
Cheque	02-Apr-2016	2	Rent		1,000.00	1,000.00
Total Richmond Real Estate					1,000.00	1,000.00
Victoria Electricity						
Cheque	19-Apr-2016	4	Electricity		176.73	176.73
Total Victoria Electricity					176.73	176.73
TOTAL					**1,632.95**	**1,632.95**

Page 1

Richmond Papers Pty Ltd
Statement of Cash Flows
April 2016

	Apr 16
OPERATING ACTIVITIES	
Net Income	9,789.79
Adjustments to reconcile Net Income	
to net cash provided by operations:	
Trade receivables	-13,670.00
Inventory Asset	-6,536.36
Trade creditors	23,550.00
Tax Payable	-863.67
Net cash provided by Operating Activities	12,269.76
INVESTING ACTIVITIES	
Motor Vehicle at Cost	-12,000.00
Motor Vehicle at Cost:Less Accum. Depr. Motor Vehicle	100.00
Net cash provided by Investing Activities	-11,900.00
FINANCING ACTIVITIES	
Owner's Capital	25,000.00
Net cash provided by Financing Activities	25,000.00
Net cash increase for period	25,369.76
Cash at end of period	**25,369.76**

Richmond Papers Pty Ltd
Trial Balance

Accrual Basis

As of April 30, 2016

	Apr 30, 16	
	Debit	Credit
Richmond Papers Pty Ltd	25,369.76	
Trade receivables	13,670.00	
Inventory Asset	6,536.36	
Undeposited Funds	0.00	
Motor Vehicle at Cost	12,000.00	
Motor Vehicle at Cost:Less Accum. Depr. Motor Vehicle		100.00
Trade creditors		23,550.00
Tax Payable	863.67	
Owner's Capital		25,000.00
Sales - A3 Copy Paper		4,363.63
Sales - A4 Copy Paper		5,559.10
Sales - A5 Copy Paper		2,163.64
Sales - Coloured Paper		3,454.55
Sales - Envelopes		3,818.18
Sales - Register Rolls		13,254.54
Cost of Goods Sold	21,090.90	
Bank Service Fee	10.00	
Depreciation – Motor Vehicle	100.00	
Electricity	176.73	
Insurance	200.00	
Rent	1,000.00	
Telephone	196.22	
Waste disposal	50.00	
TOTAL	81,263.64	81,263.64

Page 1

Richmond Papers Pty Ltd
Profit & Loss Detail
April 2016

Accrual Basis

Type	Date	Num	Name	Clr	Amount	Balance
Ordinary Income/Expense						
Income						
Sales - A3 Copy Paper						
Tax Invoice	12-Apr-2016	3	Globe Travels Pty Ltd		1,818.18	1,818.18
Tax Invoice	21-Apr-2016	6	Sally's Warehouse		2,545.45	4,363.63
Total Sales - A3 Copy Paper					4,363.63	4,363.63
Sales - A4 Copy Paper						
Tax Invoice	05-Apr-2016	1	Horizon Designs		922.73	922.73
Tax Invoice	10-Apr-2016	2	Thomson Clothings		818.18	1,740.91
Tax Invoice	12-Apr-2016	3	Globe Travels Pty Ltd		818.18	2,559.09
Tax Invoice	14-Apr-2016	4	Tiffany Cakes		681.82	3,240.91
Tax Invoice	19-Apr-2016	5	Peter Electronics		818.18	4,059.09
Tax Invoice	21-Apr-2016	6	Sally's Warehouse		954.55	5,013.64
Adjustment Note	23-Apr-2016	R2	Sally's Warehouse		-136.36	4,877.28
Tax Invoice	27-Apr-2016	8	Surf Stores		681.82	5,559.10
Total Sales - A4 Copy Paper					5,559.10	5,559.10
Sales - A5 Copy Paper						
Tax Invoice	05-Apr-2016	1	Horizon Designs		890.91	890.91
Tax Invoice	25-Apr-2016	7	Western Estate Agents		1,272.73	2,163.64
Total Sales - A5 Copy Paper					2,163.64	2,163.64
Sales - Coloured Paper						
Tax Invoice	12-Apr-2016	3	Globe Travels Pty Ltd		1,090.91	1,090.91
Tax Invoice	19-Apr-2016	5	Peter Electronics		1,272.73	2,363.64
Tax Invoice	21-Apr-2016	6	Sally's Warehouse		1,090.91	3,454.55
Total Sales - Coloured Paper					3,454.55	3,454.55
Sales - Envelopes						
Tax Invoice	10-Apr-2016	2	Thomson Clothings		2,545.45	2,545.45
Tax Invoice	14-Apr-2016	4	Tiffany Cakes		1,909.09	4,454.54
Adjustment Note	17-Apr-2016	R1	Thomson Clothings		-636.36	3,818.18
Total Sales - Envelopes					3,818.18	3,818.18
Sales - Register Rolls						
Tax Invoice	05-Apr-2016	1	Horizon Designs		2,945.45	2,945.45
Tax Invoice	12-Apr-2016	3	Globe Travels Pty Ltd		3,436.36	6,381.81
Tax Invoice	14-Apr-2016	4	Tiffany Cakes		2,945.45	9,327.26
Tax Invoice	21-Apr-2016	6	Sally's Warehouse		2,454.55	11,781.81
Tax Invoice	27-Apr-2016	8	Surf Stores		1,472.73	13,254.54
Total Sales - Register Rolls					13,254.54	13,254.54
Total Income					32,613.64	32,613.64
Cost of Goods Sold						
Cost of Goods Sold						
Tax Invoice	05-Apr-2016	1	Horizon Designs		509.09	509.09
Tax Invoice	05-Apr-2016	1	Horizon Designs		2,072.73	2,581.82
Tax Invoice	05-Apr-2016	1	Horizon Designs		509.09	3,090.91
Tax Invoice	10-Apr-2016	2	Thomson Clothings		436.36	3,527.27
Tax Invoice	10-Apr-2016	2	Thomson Clothings		1,600.00	5,127.27
Tax Invoice	12-Apr-2016	3	Globe Travels Pty Ltd		436.36	5,563.63
Tax Invoice	12-Apr-2016	3	Globe Travels Pty Ltd		1,136.36	6,699.99
Tax Invoice	12-Apr-2016	3	Globe Travels Pty Ltd		2,418.18	9,118.17
Tax Invoice	12-Apr-2016	3	Globe Travels Pty Ltd		763.64	9,881.81
Tax Invoice	14-Apr-2016	4	Tiffany Cakes		363.64	10,245.45
Tax Invoice	14-Apr-2016	4	Tiffany Cakes		2,072.73	12,318.18
Tax Invoice	14-Apr-2016	4	Tiffany Cakes		1,200.00	13,518.18
Adjustment Note	17-Apr-2016	R1	Thomson Clothings		-400.00	13,118.18
Tax Invoice	19-Apr-2016	5	Peter Electronics		436.36	13,554.54
Tax Invoice	19-Apr-2016	5	Peter Electronics		890.91	14,445.45
Tax Invoice	21-Apr-2016	6	Sally's Warehouse		509.09	14,954.54
Tax Invoice	21-Apr-2016	6	Sally's Warehouse		763.64	15,718.18
Tax Invoice	21-Apr-2016	6	Sally's Warehouse		1,590.91	17,309.09
Tax Invoice	21-Apr-2016	6	Sally's Warehouse		1,727.27	19,036.36
Adjustment Note	23-Apr-2016	R2	Sally's Warehouse		-72.73	18,963.63
Tax Invoice	25-Apr-2016	7	Western Estate Agents		727.27	19,690.90

Richmond Papers Pty Ltd
Profit & Loss Detail
Accrual Basis   April 2016

Type	Date	Num	Name	Clr	Amount	Balance
Tax Invoice	27-Apr-2016	8	Surf Stores		363.64	20,054.54
Tax Invoice	27-Apr-2016	8	Surf Stores		1,036.36	21,090.90
Total Cost of Goods Sold					21,090.90	21,090.90
Total COGS					21,090.90	21,090.90
Gross Profit					11,522.74	11,522.74
Expense						
Bank Service Fee						
Cheque	30-Apr-2016	BS	Bank of Richmond		10.00	10.00
Total Bank Service Fee					10.00	10.00
Depreciation – Motor Vehicle						
General Journal	30-Apr-2016	1			100.00	100.00
Total Depreciation – Motor Vehicle					100.00	100.00
Electricity						
Cheque	19-Apr-2016	4	Victoria Electricity		176.73	176.73
Total Electricity					176.73	176.73
Insurance						
Cheque	07-Apr-2016	3	Melbourne Insurance		200.00	200.00
Total Insurance					200.00	200.00
Rent						
Cheque	02-Apr-2016	2	Richmond Real Estate		1,000.00	1,000.00
Total Rent					1,000.00	1,000.00
Telephone						
Cheque	21-Apr-2016	5	Australia Telecom		196.22	196.22
Total Telephone					196.22	196.22
Waste disposal						
Cheque	26-Apr-2016	6	Melbourne Removals		50.00	50.00
Total Waste disposal					50.00	50.00
Total Expense					1,732.95	1,732.95
Net Ordinary Income					9,789.79	9,789.79
Net Income					**9,789.79**	**9,789.79**

Richmond Papers Pty Ltd
Balance Sheet
As of April 30, 2016

Accrual Basis

	Apr 30, 16
ASSETS	
Current Assets	
Chequing/Savings	
Richmond Papers Pty Ltd	25,369.76
Total Chequing/Savings	25,369.76
Accounts Receivable	
Trade receivables	13,670.00
Total Accounts Receivable	13,670.00
Other Current Assets	
Inventory Asset	6,536.36
Total Other Current Assets	6,536.36
Total Current Assets	45,576.12
Fixed Assets	
Motor Vehicle at Cost	
Less Accum. Depr. Motor Vehicle	-100.00
Motor Vehicle at Cost - Other	12,000.00
Total Motor Vehicle at Cost	11,900.00
Total Fixed Assets	11,900.00
TOTAL ASSETS	**57,476.12**
LIABILITIES	
Current Liabilities	
Accounts Payable	
Trade creditors	23,550.00
Total Accounts Payable	23,550.00
Other Current Liabilities	
Tax Payable	-863.67
Total Other Current Liabilities	-863.67
Total Current Liabilities	22,686.33
TOTAL LIABILITIES	**22,686.33**
NET ASSETS	**34,789.79**
EQUITY	
Owner's Capital	25,000.00
Net Income	9,789.79
TOTAL EQUITY	**34,789.79**

www.ingramcontent.com/pod-product-compliance
Lightning Source LLC
Chambersburg PA
CBHW060514060326
40689CB00020B/4741